Let's get Zapping!

So what should you be zapping in the Annual?

Wherever you see the interactive icon you'll be able to unlock a fun experience to enjoy on your device. There are seven scattered throughout the Annual and one on the front cover to discover.

See if you can find them all.

Ready

Open Zappar on your device.

Aim

Scan the code on the page.

Zap

Then point your device at the page and watch it come to life!

A few helpful tips...

- Connect to wifi if you can and the experiences will download even quicker than on 3G.
- Try and keep the pages as flat as you can for the best effect. Rest the Annual on a table or on the floor.
- Try and keep the full page in view from your phone after scanning the code. Don't get too close or far away if you can help it.

To get the best possible experience here are a few hints and tips:

- Try and keep the pages clean and free from tears, pen and other marks as this may affect the experience.
- It's best to view the pages in good lighting conditions if you can.

If you're still having problems then do contact us at support@zappar.com and we'll do our best to help you.

CONTENTS

WELCOME

Listen up, Hulkamaniacs! You know the Hulkster never backs down from a challenge, but I think even I need a little help here. This amazing Annual is loaded with activities, quizzes and challenges bigger than the one I had when I faced Andre the Giant at *WrestleMania III*! And if that isn't enough, dudes and dudettes, we've also got exclusive, in-depth profiles on enough Superstars to fill up a *Royal Rumble*!

Ready for more? Because we've got the lowdown on some of *WrestleMania XXXI*'s biggest matches and moments! When you've conquered this Annual, maniacs, you're going to be ready to run WWE!

So, let me ask you, brother... whatcha gonna do when the WWE Annual runs wild on you??

Hulk Hogan

Pedigree

Published 2015. Pedigree Books Ltd, Beech Hill House, Walnut Gardens, Exeter, Devon EX4 4DH
books@pedigreegroup.co.uk – www.pedigreebooks.com

The Pedigree trademark, email and website addresses, are the sole and exclusive properties of Pedigree Group Limited, used under licence in this publication.

JOHN CENA

SUPERSTAR STATS

Height: 6ft 1in **Weight:** 251 lbs
From: West Newbury, Mass.
Signature Moves: Attitude Adjustment; STF

If there's one thing anyone can say about John Cena, it's that he knows how to win. Even a loss like the one he suffered against Brock Lesnar at the 2014 *SummerSlam* isn't enough to keep him down. Cena knows that being a true winner doesn't mean coming out on top every time. It means having the strength to get back up when you're down and get back in the fight. That's why, win or lose, John Cena will remain one of WWE's greatest champions of all time.

MANIA FACT:
John Cena won or retained a championship at his first five consecutive *WrestleMania* matches!

RUSEV

MANIA FACT:
The Super Athelete's first *WrestleMania* match was for the United States Title against John Cena. That's the same title Cena competed for at his first *WrestleMania*!

SUPERSTAR STATS

Height: 6ft 0in **Weight:** 138kg
From: Russia
Signature Moves: The Accolade

Rusev is a Superstar born and bred to conquer. His size, strength and sheer power is matched only by his dislike for other competitors. He likes nothing more than to trap his opponents in his Accolade finishing move and remind them just who the toughest and strongest Superstar on the roster is. For nearly a year, Rusev dominated all who crossed his path while his manager, Lana, reveled in telling spectators how inferior their heroes are to the Super Athlete. Everyone is hoping that someday, someone will prove them both wrong!

ROMAN REIGNS

SUPERSTAR STATS

Height: 6ft 3in   **Weight:** 265 lbs
From: Pensacola, Fla.
Signature Moves: Spear; Superman Punch

After winning the 2015 *Royal Rumble*, Roman Reigns has risen to the top of the list of WWE's most powerful players! His brutal Spear and powerful Superman Punch are a lethal one-two combo that have taken out competitors ranging from Big Show to Daniel Bryan to The Authority itself. Roman is on a one-way trip to the top and anyone who gets in his way is going to get mowed down!

MANIA FACT:

Roman Reigns, along with his former Shield-mates, won both of their matches at *WrestleMania XXIX* and *WrestleMania 30*. If not for his wayward former friend, Seth Rollins, Roman could have been 3-0 at the Show of Shows!

BROCK LESNAR

SUPERSTAR STATS

Height: 6ft 3in   **Weight:** 286 lbs
From: Minneapolis, Minn.
Signature Moves: F-5; Kimura Lock

Like WWE Hall of Famer Arnold Schwarzenegger's Terminator, Brock Lesnar is a machine bent on total destruction. He doesn't feel pity. He doesn't feel pain. He only knows how to destroy. Undertaker learned that lesson well in 2014 when The Beast pinned him at *WrestleMania 30* to end The Streak after 21 years. Lesnar continues to come back and dish out more punishment than most Superstars are willing to take. You can't stop him, but you're welcome to try!

MANIA FACT:

Before his return to WWE in 2012, Brock's last appearance was at *WrestleMania XX!*

WWE WRESTLEMANIA

REIGNS VS LESNAR

Roman Reigns won the *Royal Rumble* Match and earned himself a shot at the WWE World Heavyweight Championship. But in order to walk out of *WrestleMania* with the Title, he was going to have to defeat the Beast himself, Brock Lesnar. Roman was ready for a fight, but the night had surprises in store even he couldn't have predicted!

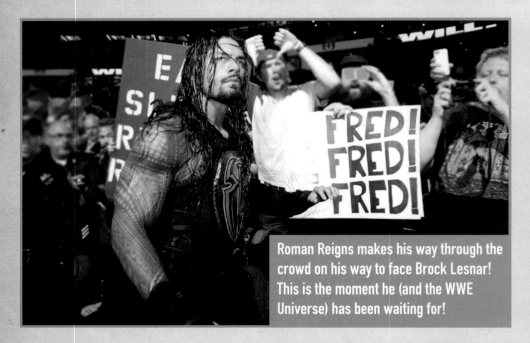

Roman Reigns makes his way through the crowd on his way to face Brock Lesnar! This is the moment he (and the WWE Universe) has been waiting for!

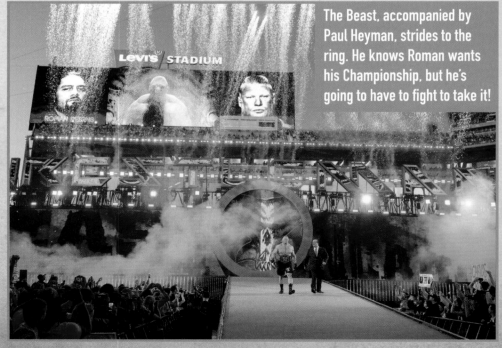

The Beast, accompanied by Paul Heyman, strides to the ring. He knows Roman wants his Championship, but he's going to have to fight to take it!

It's on! Reigns earned his title shot at the *Royal Rumble*, and now he's here to take the gold!

WrestleMania may be in Santa Clara, but Lesnar is taking Roman to Suplex City.

The Beast hits an F–5 on Roman...and doesn't even attempt the pinfall. He just wants to send a message to Roman. He's in for a night of pain!

Boom! Brock takes the fight to Roman again and again! The only question is... how long can Roman hold on?

After being nailed by the ring post, Lesnar is stunned and Roman has his chance! He takes Brock down with a hard-hitting Superman Punch!

Roman's on the attack! Lesnar has been knocked for a loop and Roman may just be able to become the new champion!

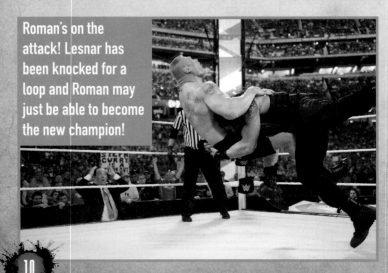

Lesnar is down! Can Roman take advantage of the moment and put him away for good?

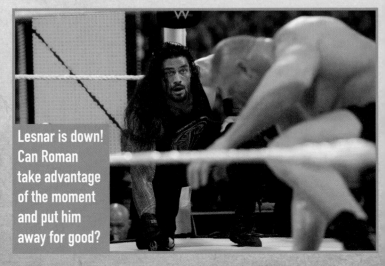

Spear! Spear! Spear! Lesnar is taken to the mat again! This is it!

Not yet! Lesnar still has some fight left in him and hits Roman with another F-5! Could this one put him away for good?

Lesnar grabs Reigns and sets him up for a fourth F-5! Paul Heyman laughs evilly. This could be it!

What's this? Seth Rollins is coming out to the ring? What does he have planned? Could he be...

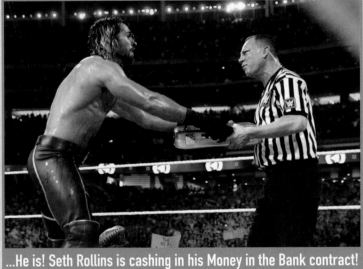

...He is! Seth Rollins is cashing in his Money in the Bank contract!

It's official! Seth Rollins has cashed in his contract and we have a Triple Threat Match on our hands!

Seth goes right on the attack, hitting a Curb Stomp on Lesnar. Can he put the Beast away?

Brock has Seth right where he wants him! This could be the end!

A Spear from Roman Reigns takes out both Seth and Lesnar!

Too late, Roman! Seth jumps in and nails Reigns with a Curb Stomp for the win!

He did it! Seth Rollins has pinned Roman Reigns to win the gold!

Roman lies defeated, but we know he'll be back! And Seth Rollins had better watch out!

The battle has left the Beast weary. His advocate, Paul Heyman, wonders if he'll be OK!

Brock has been beaten, but we know that he generally prefers to give beatings. Who's next?

We have a new WWE World Heavyweight Champion! Seth Rollins shocked the WWE Universe and his opponents! What will he do next?

BECOME THE CHAMP!

Making it all the way to the top in WWE takes talent, determination and a lot of luck! Think you have what it takes? You have to be ready to roll with the punches and face whatever setbacks come your way. If you can do that...then you might be championship material!

WHAT YOU NEED
2 PLAYERS
1 OR 2 DICE
COUNTERS OR COINS

START HERE

8
Sprain your ankle doing a moonsault. Out for a week. **MISS A TURN.**

9

10
Promotion to WWE Roster. **MOVE FORWARD 2 SPACES**

7
Win your first match. **ROLL AGAIN**

35

36

6

34
Eliminated by El Torito. **MOVE BACK TO SPACE 24**

5
Earn a tryout match on *SmackDown*. **MOVE TO 12**

33

SMACK DOWN

32
WWE **ROYAL RUMBLE**

4

3

31
Dropped for a Gimmick Battle Royal. **GO BACK 5 SPACES**

2
Trip on your way to the ring at an *NXT: Takeover event*. Go back to the start!

30

1
NXT

29
Your big win on Raw lands you a spot in the Royal Rumble Match. **MOVE FORWARD 3 SPACES.**

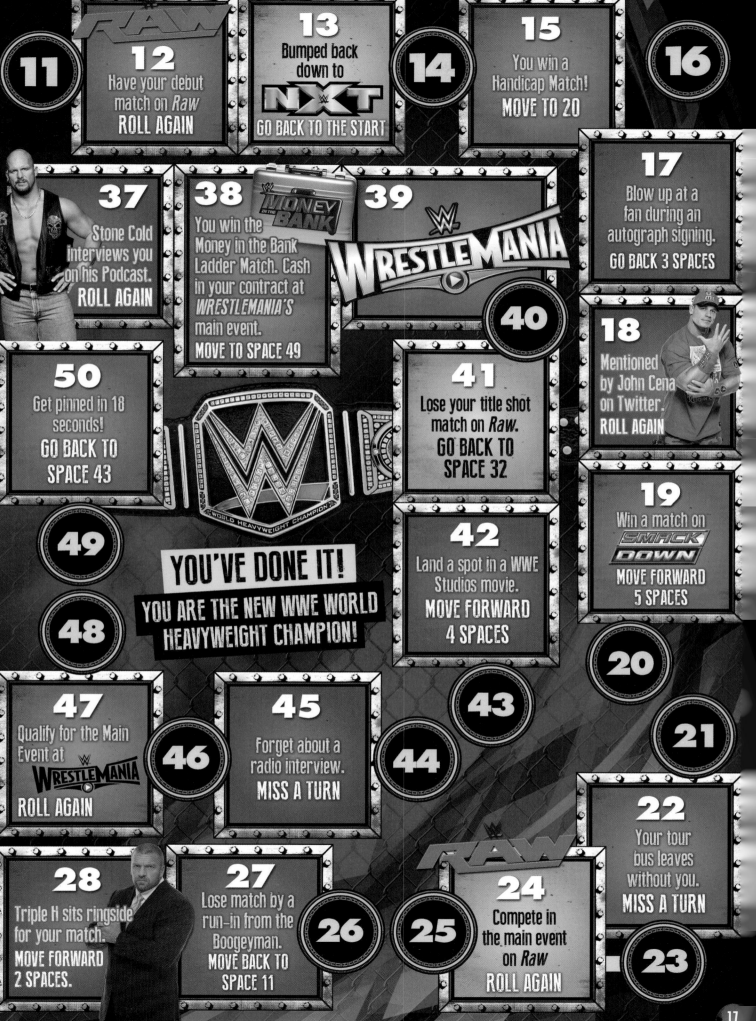

11

12
Have your debut match on *Raw*
ROLL AGAIN

13
Bumped back down to
NXT
GO BACK TO THE START

14

15
You win a Handicap Match!
MOVE TO 20

16

17
Blow up at a fan during an autograph signing.
GO BACK 3 SPACES

37
Stone Cold interviews you on his Podcast.
ROLL AGAIN

38
You win the Money in the Bank Ladder Match. Cash in your contract at *WRESTLEMANIA'S* main event.
MOVE TO SPACE 49

39
WRESTLEMANIA

40

18
Mentioned by John Cena on Twitter.
ROLL AGAIN

50
Get pinned in 18 seconds!
GO BACK TO SPACE 43

41
Lose your title shot match on *Raw*.
GO BACK TO SPACE 32

19
Win a match on
SMACK DOWN
MOVE FORWARD 5 SPACES

49

42
Land a spot in a WWE Studios movie.
MOVE FORWARD 4 SPACES

48

YOU'VE DONE IT!
YOU ARE THE NEW WWE WORLD HEAVYWEIGHT CHAMPION!

43

20

47
Qualify for the Main Event at
WRESTLEMANIA
ROLL AGAIN

46

45
Forget about a radio interview.
MISS A TURN

44

21

22
Your tour bus leaves without you.
MISS A TURN

28
Triple H sits ringside for your match.
MOVE FORWARD 2 SPACES.

27
Lose match by a run-in from the Boogeyman.
MOVE BACK TO SPACE 11

26

25

24
Compete in the main event on *Raw*
ROLL AGAIN

23

WWE BIG QUIZ

PART ONE

Are you an expert of all things WWE? Try your hand at these tough questions and see if you're Superstar material!

QUESTION 01

WHICH OF THESE CITIES HAS NEVER HOSTED A *WRESTLEMANIA*?

- New York ☐
- Houston ☐
- San Diego ☐
- Indianapolis ☐

QUESTION 02

WHO DEFEATED TRIPLE H ON THE 9/14/99 *SMACKDOWN* TO WIN HIS FIRST (AND ONLY) WWE CHAMPIONSHIP?

- Big Show ☐
- John Cena ☐
- Batista ☐
- Mr. McMahon ☐

QUESTION 03

WHICH ONE OF UNDERTAKER'S 21 *WRESTLEMANIA* WINS WAS NOT A RESULT OF PINFALL OR SUBMISSION?

- *WrestleMania XX* against Kane ☐
- *WrestleMania IX* against Giant Gonzalez ☐
- *WrestleMania XV* against Big Bossman ☐
- *WrestleMania X8* against Ric Flair ☐

QUESTION 04

WHICH EVIL GROUP WAS DANIEL BRYAN FORMERLY A MEMBER OF?

- DX ☐
- Evolution ☐
- The Nexus ☐
- La Familia ☐

QUESTION 05

WHO DID RIC FLAIR FACE IN HIS FINAL MATCH IN WWE?

- Shawn Michaels ☐
- Triple H ☐
- Randy Orton ☐
- Batista ☐

QUESTION 06

WHAT IS TRIPLE H'S CURRENT POSITION IN WWE?

- COO ☐
- CEO ☐
- CFO ☐
- CPA ☐

QUESTION 07

WHICH OF THESE MATCHES IS NOT A REAL WWE MATCH?

- Coal Miner's Glove match ☐
- Hands Off the Top Rope Match ☐
- Crybaby Match ☐
- Kiss My Foot Match ☐

QUESTION 08

WHO IS THE LONGEST-REIGNING INTERCONTINENTAL CHAMPION?

- Chris Jericho ☐
- Dean Ambrose ☐
- Dolph Ziggler ☐
- Honky Tonk Man ☐

QUESTION 09

BRAY WYATT TELLS HIS FOLLOWERS TO "FOLLOW THE...

- Crows ☐
- Sheep ☐
- Sparrows ☐
- Buzzards ☐

QUESTION 10

WHICH SUPERSTAR WAS NOT A MEMBER OF EVOLUTION?

- Batista ☐
- Randy Orton ☐
- Seth Rollins ☐
- Ric Flair ☐

QUESTION 11

DAMIEN SANDOW FORMERLY WORKED AS THE MIZ'S...

- Bodyguard ☐
- Hype Man ☐
- Personal Trainer ☐
- Stunt Double ☐

QUESTION 12

BY THE END OF 2014, HOW MANY TIMES HAD JOHN CENA BEEN A WORLD CHAMPION?

- 12 times ☐
- 18 times ☐
- 15 times ☐
- 21 times ☐

QUESTION 13

WHAT ARE THE ONLY TWO WAYS A SUPERSTAR CAN WIN A TITLE IN WWE?

- Pinfall or DQ ☐
- Pinfall or countout ☐
- Pinfall or forfeit ☐
- Pinfall or submission ☐

QUESTION 14

HALL OF FAME

WHO WAS THE FIRST WWE SUPERSTAR INDUCTED INTO THE WWE HALL OF FAME?

- Hulk Hogan ☐
- Andre the Giant ☐
- Bruno Sammartino ☐
- Ultimate Warrior ☐

QUESTION 15

ROMAN REIGNS IS A MEMBER OF WHAT FAMOUS WRESTLING FAMILY?

- Anoa'i ☐
- Guerrero ☐
- Hart ☐
- McMahon ☐

QUESTION 16

AT 589 POUNDS, WHO IS THE HEAVIEST SUPERSTAR TO EVER HOLD THE WWE CHAMPIONSHIP?

- Andre the Giant ☐
- Big Show ☐
- Yokozuna ☐
- The Great Khali ☐

QUESTION 17

AT THE 2015 *ROYAL RUMBLE*, WHOSE RECORD DID KANE BREAK FOR MOST CAREER ELIMINATIONS?

- Bret Hart ☐
- Edge ☐
- The Rock ☐
- Shawn Michaels ☐

QUESTION 18

WHO IS THE ONLY SUPERSTAR TO FACE UNDERTAKER THREE TIMES AT *WRESTLEMANIA*?

- Kane ☐
- Triple H ☐
- Randy Orton ☐
- Big Show ☐

QUESTION 19

WHICH 2015 HALL OF FAMER PLAYED A WRESTLER WHO BATTLED PETER PARKER IN 2002'S *SPIDER-MAN* MOVIE?

- Rikishi ☐
- Arnold ☐
- Randy Savage ☐
- Alundra Blayze ☐

QUESTION 20

WHO DID DOLPH ZIGGLER CASH IN HIS MONEY IN THE BANK CONTRACT ON TO WIN HIS FIRST WORLD TITLE?

- Big Show ☐
- Jack Swagger ☐
- Sheamus ☐
- Alberto Del Rio ☐

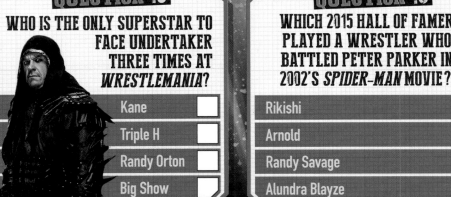

Awesome job! But, just like Daniel Bryan at *WrestleMania 30*, winning once isn't enough! Turn to page 34 for your next challenge. Can you do it? Yes! Yes! Yes!

BRIE BELLA

SUPERSTAR STATS
Height: 5ft 6in   **From:** Scottsdale, Ariz.

Following a nasty rivalry with her twin sister Nikki, Brie kissed and made up with her sibling and the two reunited to become stronger than ever. With the help of "Brie Mode", Nikki overpowered AJ Lee at *Survivor Series* to become Divas Champion. Since then, the two have become a powerful force in WWE, taking out anyone who dares to challenge them. The only question is, how long can it last?

MANIA FACT:
The Bellas were supposed to compete at *WrestleMania 29*, but their match was cancelled because of time constraints.

Fearless NIKKI

SUPERSTAR STATS
Height: 5ft 6in
From: San Diego, Calif.

Nikki Bella went from WWE Diva to TV celebrity to Divas Champion, and she did it her own way. Feisty and fearless, with just a hint of ruthlessness, Nikki Bella is unafraid to make enemies on her way to the top. And that's just what she did when she united with her sister Brie to defeat AJ Lee for the Divas Title at *Survivor Series*. Some people were stunned, but Nikki's not here to make friends. That's what sisters are for!

PAIGE

SUPERSTAR STATS

Height: 5ft 8in
From: Norwich, England.
Signature Moves: Paige-Turner; Ram-Paige; PTO (Paige Tapout)

Paige comes from a wrestling family, and it was this skill that catapulted her to one of the most shocking debuts in WWE history. When AJ challenged her to a title match on the spot, Paige accepted...and won! Of course, now that people have seen what this British Diva can do, the upset victory should come as no surprise. Paige knows how to fight and anyone who gets in her way had better be ready to put up or get put down!

MANIA FACT:
Paige's first match was the day after *WrestleMania 30*, where she became the youngest Divas Champion ever!

NAOMI

SUPERSTAR STATS

Height: 5ft 5in
From: Orlando, Fla.

Once one of the dancers who accompanied the Funkasaurus Brodus Clay, Naomi has begun to carve out her own place in WWE. As the star of Total Divas, Naomi and her former tag partner Cameron turned stardom in the WWE ring into stardom on the small screen. Unfortunately, her partnership with Cameron came to an end, but Naomi's been doing just fine on her own. She helped her team score the win at *Survivor Series* and is definitely ready for big things in 2015!

MANIA FACT:
Naomi made her *WrestleMania* debut at *WrestleMania XXVIII* as one of the Funkadactyls dancing with Brodus Clay and an entire chorus line of dancing mamas!

SUPERSTAR NAME GENERATOR

If you want to be a WWE Superstar, the first thing you'll need is a name! Problem is, all the good ones are taken! Let us help you out! Follow these steps and your new name will be in lights in no time!

FIRST LETTER OF YOUR FIRST NAME

A	Amazing
B	Brutal
C	Charismatic
D	Dashing
E	Enigmatic
F	Fresh
G	Gigantic
H	Hilarious
I	Intense
J	Jaw-Dropping
K	Kinetic
L	Locomotive
M	Maniacal
N	Nightmarish
O	Odd
P	Phantasmagoric
Q	Quarrelsome
R	Rabid
S	Sizzling
T	Terrifying
U	Unforgiving
V	Valiant
W	Warlike
X	X-treme
Y	Yucky
Z	Zesty

FIRST LETTER OF YOUR SURNAME

A	Anaconda
B	Banshee
C	Carnivore
D	Demon
E	Eel
F	Fox
G	Gorilla
H	Hunter
I	Invader
J	Jackal
K	Knight
L	Lionfish
M	Mauler
N	Nightcrawler
O	Octopus
P	Pit Viper
Q	Quinotaur
R	Razorback
S	Sidewinder
T	Tornado
U	Unknown
V	Vanquisher
W	Wizard
X	X-Ray
Y	Yo-Yo
Z	Zookeeper

MY SUPERSTAR NAME IS...

FROM THE OFFICE OF...

THE AUTHORITY

The Authority are making some notes on their favourite (and least favourite) Superstars! Can you guess who they are talking about just from their comments?

1. Smart guy. Chooses his friends wisely.
Knows how to make the most of an opportunity.
Futuristic ring gear. I like it. Progressive!
Couldn't he pick one colour for his hair?

SUPERSTAR: ....

2. Knows how to get the fans behind him.
Hijacked Raw one time. Not cool!
Wrestled twice at WrestleMania 30. Impressive.
LOSE THE BEARD!

SUPERSTAR: ....

3. Hard-hitting finisher.
Bare-knuckle fighter. That's tough!
Preston North End fan. Hmmm...
Can't he deliver good news for once?

SUPERSTAR: ....

4. Spooky entrance. Really creepy music.
What's he saying most of the time?
That backwards walking thing is scary!
Anyone who faces Undertaker at WrestleMania is OK in my book...

SUPERSTAR: ....

5. One of the biggest daredevils on the roster!
Almost beat John Cena for the US Title!
Longest reigning US Champion in history. Impressive.
Is he really insane???

SUPERSTAR: ....

6. WWE Superstar AND movie star.
Former football player with the University of Miami.
Always good at coming up with catchphrases.
Almost ruined our WrestleMania moment!

SUPERSTAR: ....

7. Used to be a good friend.
Won the Royal Rumble in 2009.
3rd Generation Superstar.
Beat our "Plan B" at WrestleMania.

SUPERSTAR: ....

8. Hard-hitting finisher.
Almost beat Triple H at WrestleMania. Almost!
Maybe too pale?
Kind of liking the new look.

SUPERSTAR: ....

SUPERSTAR

| HEAD **JOHN CENA** | HEAD **ROMAN REIGNS** | HEAD **BRAY WYATT** | HEAD **STARDUST** |

SHIRT

TRUNKS

BOOTS

SHIRT

TRUNKS

BOOTS

SHIRT

TRUNKS

BOOTS

SHIRT

TRUNKS

BOOTS

SWAP

HEAD
SETH ROLLINS

HEAD
RYBACK

HEAD
SHEAMUS

HEAD
ADAM ROSE

SHIRT

TRUNKS

BOOTS

SHIRT

TRUNKS

BOOTS

SHIRT

TRUNKS

BOOTS

SHIRT

TRUNKS

BOOTS

DANIEL BRYAN

SUPERSTAR STATS

Height: 5ft 10in **Weight:** 210 lbs
From: Aberdeen, WA. **Signature Move:** "Yes!" Lock

Life hasn't been easy for Daniel Bryan this past year. After winning the WWE World Heavyweight Championship at *WrestleMania 30*, he was sidelined by an injury and forced to sit out the rest of the year. He's had a tough battle since his comeback at the 2015 *Royal Rumble*, but really, when hasn't Daniel had a tough battle? From day one, Daniel's been fighting his way to the top and we're guessing he'll be fighting until he hangs up his boots for good.

MANIA FACT:

Daniel Bryan lost to Sheamus at *WrestleMania XXVIII* in 18 seconds, but Bryan has redeemed himself with three consecutive *WrestleMania* wins with three different Titles on the line.

#BNB

MANIA FACT:

Despite being in WWE for nearly five years, Bad News has yet to win a match at the Show of Shows!

SUPERSTAR STATS

Height: 6ft 7in **Weight:** 246 lbs
From: Preston, England
Signature Moves: Bad News Bull Hammer Elbow

Bad News Barrett loves nothing more than ruining people's days. For a while he was just doing it with his words, but lately he's also been doing it with his fists! His Bull Hammer Elbow has proven powerful enough to take out Superstars ranging from the likes of Big Show to Dolph Ziggler, from whom Barrett won the Intercontinental Championship. As far as Barrett's concerned, there's no news like Bad News!

UNDERTAKER

SUPERSTAR STATS

Height: 6ft 10in **Weight:** 299 lbs
From: Death Valley
Signature Moves: Chokeslam; Tombstone; Last Ride

There have been many Superstars and many Legends, but there is only one Deadman. Even when a stunning loss to Brock Lesnar at *WrestleMania 30* broke his winning streak, Undertaker didn't stay down. He returned with lightning and thunder to face and defeat Bray Wyatt at *WrestleMania 31*. Twenty-five years after he first arose, Undertaker still haunts the WWE roster. It just goes to show, you can't keep a Deadman down!

MANIA FACT:
Undertaker's match against King Kong Bundy at *WrestleMania XI* was actually refereed by a baseball umpire!

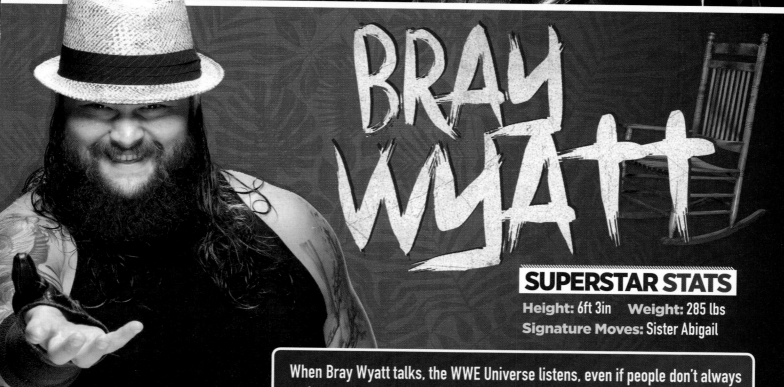

BRAY WYATT

MANIA FACT:
Bray Wyatt was the first Superstar to face Undertaker at *WrestleMania* (or any event) since the ending of The Streak at *WrestleMania 30*.

SUPERSTAR STATS

Height: 6ft 3in **Weight:** 285 lbs
Signature Moves: Sister Abigail

When Bray Wyatt talks, the WWE Universe listens, even if people don't always understand what he's saying. His crazy speeches and demented ramblings captivate audiences and terrify Superstars alike. But Bray is more than just talk. He can back it all up with his in-ring ability and his devastating Sister Abigail finisher. Time will tell if Bray can find more followers to do his bidding. If that happens, everyone had better watch their backs!

WrestleMania

UNDERTAKER VS WYATT

The Phenom hadn't been seen anywhere in WWE since losing to Brock Lesnar at *WrestleMania 30*. But Bray Wyatt had decided to call him back from the beyond to face him in a once-in-a-lifetime showdown on the Grandest Stage of Them All. Bray taunted and tempted the Deadman, daring him to face him at *WrestleMania*. And when the match finally happened, it was total excitement like only the Deadman could deliver!

Bray Wyatt comes down the ramp with an army of shambling scarecrows. Super creepy!"

The fog is rolling, the bells are tolling! Undertaker is back!

The Deadman's been gone a year, but he's as tough as ever!

Undertaker goes up top for Old School! Bray's in for a real fight tonight!

Bray battles back! He sends the Deadman over the top rope with a vicious clothesline!

Bray's down again as the Phenom unleashes a leg drop that will put Bray away for good!

The Deadman traps Bray in Hell's Gate! Can the Eater of Worlds make his escape?

Bray's not out of the fight yet! He nails Undertaker with Sister Abigail!

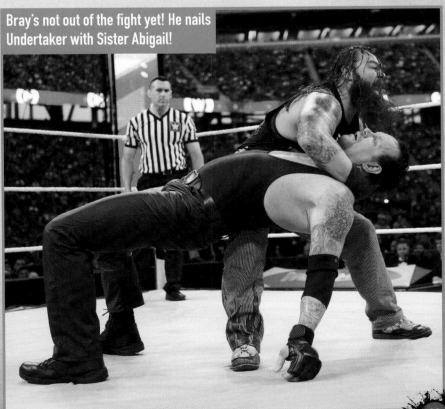

1!. . .2!. . .

No good! The Deadman kicks out and the battle goes on!

He can't pin the Deadman, but can Bray get inside his mind? He tries to creep him out with his ultra-scary spider walk!

The Deadman isn't buying it! He sits back up and stares right into Bray's eyes!

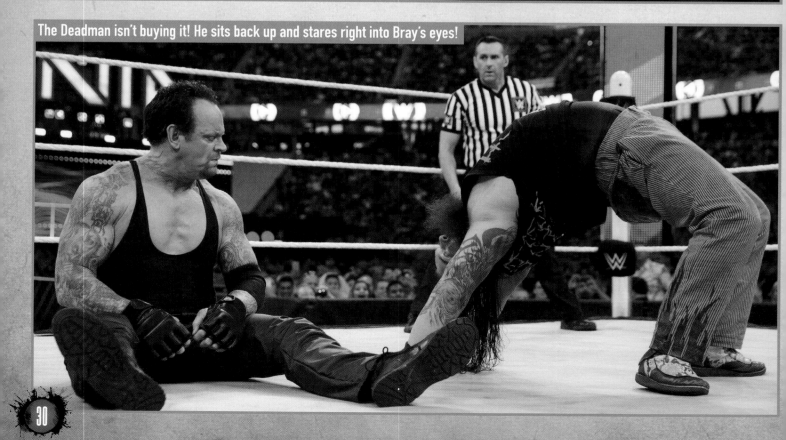

Uh-oh! Bray has looked into the eyes of the Deadman, and he doesn't like what he sees!

The Deadman claims another victim!

Tombstone! This could be the end for Bray!

Victory is his! Once again, *WrestleMania* belongs to Undertaker!

VAULTS OF THE UNDERTAKER

THE DEADMAN HAS CHANGED HIS LOOK MANY TIMES OVER THE YEARS, ALL YOU HAVE TO DO IS MATCH THE PERSONA TO THE YEAR HE WORE IT TO THE RING.

MANY HAVE TRIED!

& FAILED

LORD OF DARKNESS

BIG EVIL

THE LAST OUTLAW

MINISTER OF EVIL

WRESTLEMANIA XIV

MORTICIAN

CHOOSE FROM THESE YEARS

1990 1994

1995 1996

1998 1999

2001 2003

2004 2013

DON'T BE AFRAID BE TERRIFIED

RETURN OF THE DEADMAN

ORIGINAL DEADMAN

THE PHANTOM

AMERICAN BADASS

CHECK YOUR ANSWERS IF YOU DARE ON PAGE 60

WWE BIG QUIZ

PART TWO

TIME TO PUT YOUR THINKING CAPS ON AND SEE IF YOU CAN SORT OUT THE FACTS FROM THE FAKES!

QUESTION 01
JOHN CENA IS A TWO-TIME INTERCONTINENTAL CHAMPION.

TRUE ☐   FALSE ☐

QUESTION 02

ROMAN REIGNS IS THE ROCK'S COUSIN.

TRUE ☐   FALSE ☐

QUESTION 03
THERE HAS NEVER BEEN A *WRESTLEMANIA* HELD OUTSIDE THE U.S.

TRUE ☐   FALSE ☐

QUESTION 04
BROCK LESNAR'S DEFEAT OF JOHN CENA WAS HIS FIRST WORLD TITLE WIN.

TRUE ☐   FALSE ☐

QUESTION 05

SHEAMUS IS THE FIRST IRISH-BORN WWE CHAMPION.

TRUE ☐   FALSE ☐

QUESTION 06
MR. MCMAHON IS A FORMER ECW CHAMPION.

TRUE ☐   FALSE ☐

QUESTION 07

STING IS A ONE-TIME WWE CHAMPION.

TRUE ☐   FALSE ☐

QUESTION 08

AJ LEE ONCE MET LITA AT AN AUTOGRAPH SIGNING.

TRUE ☐   FALSE ☐

QUESTION 09

ANDRE THE GIANT ONCE PLAYED BIGFOOT ON TV.

TRUE ☐　FALSE ☐

QUESTION 10

EVERY MEMBER OF THE MCMAHON FAMILY HAS HELD A TITLE IN WWE.

TRUE ☐　FALSE ☐

QUESTION 11

BIG SHOW IS A TRAINED BOXER.

TRUE ☐　FALSE ☐

QUESTION 12

DANIEL BRYAN IS THE FIRST SUPERSTAR TO WRESTLE MORE THAN ONCE AT THE SAME *WRESTLEMANIA*.

TRUE ☐　FALSE ☐

QUESTION 13

CHRIS JERICHO WON THE INTERCONTINENTAL CHAMPIONSHIP TEN TIMES.

TRUE ☐　FALSE ☐

QUESTION 14

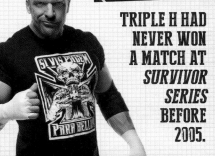

TRIPLE H HAD NEVER WON A MATCH AT *SURVIVOR SERIES* BEFORE 2005.

TRUE ☐　FALSE ☐

QUESTION 15

BO DALLAS AND PAIGE ARE THE FIRST WWE SUPERSTARS TO BE BORN IN THE 90s.

TRUE ☐　FALSE ☐

QUESTION 16

RIC FLAIR WON THE WWE TITLE AND THE *ROYAL RUMBLE* IN THE SAME NIGHT.

TRUE ☐　FALSE ☐

QUESTION 17

THE FIRST CAGE MATCH WAS HELD IN 1937.

TRUE ☐　FALSE ☐

QUESTION 18

DANIEL BRYAN IS A STRICT VEGETARIAN.

TRUE ☐　FALSE ☐

QUESTION 19

GOLDUST IS YET TO WIN A MATCH AT *WRESTLEMANIA*.

TRUE ☐　FALSE ☐

QUESTION 20

THE ROCK ONCE PLAYED HIS FATHER, ROCKY JOHNSON, ON TV.

TRUE ☐　FALSE ☐

Nice job! You should be proud of yourself! But your real challenge is still ahead. Turn to page 54 for the last, and toughest quiz yet!

SUPERSTAR WORDSEARCH

We've hidden a Battle Royal's worth of Superstar nicknames and finishing moves amongst these random letters. **Can you discover them?**

NICKNAMES

- RATTLESNAKE
- PEOPLE'S CHAMP
- LUNATIC FRINGE
- DEADMAN
- EATER OF WORLDS
- HULKSTER
- ANIMAL
- SUPER ATHLETE
- AWESOME
- BIG DOG
- SHOWOFF
- VIPER
- BIG RED MONSTER
- CELTIC WARRIOR

MOVES

- LEG DROP
- CHOKESLAM
- STUNNER
- SISTER ABIGAIL
- FIGURE FOUR
- RKO
- DIRTY DEEDS
- SPEAR
- ROCK BOTTOM
- TOMBSTONE
- BROGUE KICK
- ZIG ZAG
- BATISTA BOMB
- ACCOLADE

X P E M L Y P N B N T Z R L E R T W F B
S I E T O E U I D E G O M S M T L J P C
K D Y O A T G T B I I Y A D O J R I G M
T J L M P D T D O R W R L E S N E D H R
U O S R O L R O R L Y E X E E D T L A H
N D M G O N E A B O V B O D W R S X K L
M A Z B P W W S U K P Y H Y A X N I A B
T T M G S C F D C O C H N T B U O X I R
C Z K D I T B O X H V O T R O C M A C Y
B A N T A S O F R R A L R I L H D A U N
C C L H X E N N O E E M B D J O E N E V
Z E R S A A D L E S T P P J K K R I Y O
C S T U N N E R N A G A I R O E G M M M
R P T P Y B F A E D A V E V Y S I A I R
A K Z E T F K E D A L O C C A L B L U H
E A W R M E B M O B A T S I T A B O U K
P R L A B R O U G E K I C K H M F L K T
S I S T E R A B I G A I L F E E K K O A
J Z L H G A Z G I Z O K F H R S M Z W Z
Q D W L V P R Y Q E F O Y U T I R M C G
X X R E B E K O J P W J G E G Z U U B I
O C N T C C P F Y O E I R O M Y V Y Z S
F Y T E F O T F H N O Y A C B B F C Q
Z T Y X R D L S U J L Q Z P N L Y X H D
W N T H A I E G N I R F C I T A N U L Q

EXTRA CHALLENGE

Great job! Now, for an extra challenge, can you match the finishing move to the Superstars' nickname?

ANSWERS ON PAGE 60

stardust

SUPERSTAR STATS

Height: 6ft 2in **Weight:** 220 lbs
From: Marietta, GA.
Signature Move: Dark Matter

Stardust is easily one of the strangest Superstars ever to appear in a WWE ring, and that's part of why the WWE Universe is captivated by him! His partnership with Goldust netted him the "cosmic key" (AKA the WWE Tag Team Titles), but ended in disaster when the two split up. No one can predict what Stardust has in store, but it's a safe bet that it's going to be weird!

MANIA FACT:
Stardust (competing as his previous self) lost to Big Show at *WrestleMania XXVIII*, ending an Intercontinental Title reign of 236 days!

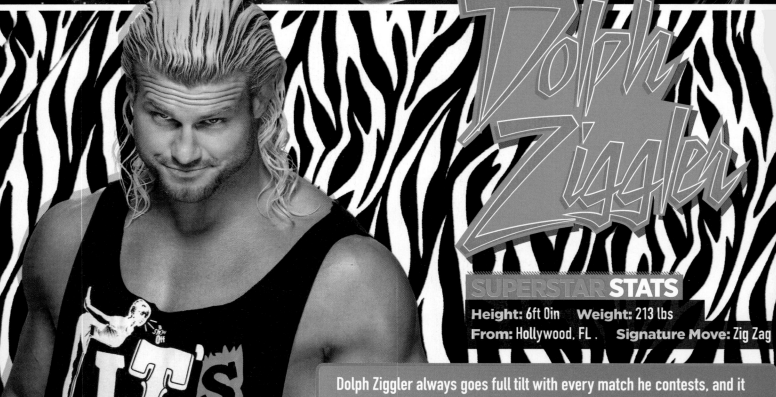

Dolph Ziggler

SUPERSTAR STATS

Height: 6ft 0in **Weight:** 213 lbs
From: Hollywood, FL . **Signature Move:** Zig Zag

MANIA FACT:
Dolph's *WrestleMania* debut was in the Money in the Bank Ladder Match at *WrestleMania XXVI*.

Dolph Ziggler always goes full tilt with every match he contests, and it was that intensity that helped him defeat Seth Rollins to give Team Cena the victory at *Survivor Series* and sent him to the top of the ladder to claim the Intercontinental Championship at WWE TLC. Although he lost it a month later to Bad News Barrett, Ziggler doesn't know the word "quit," and it won't be long before he's back on top again!

Triple H

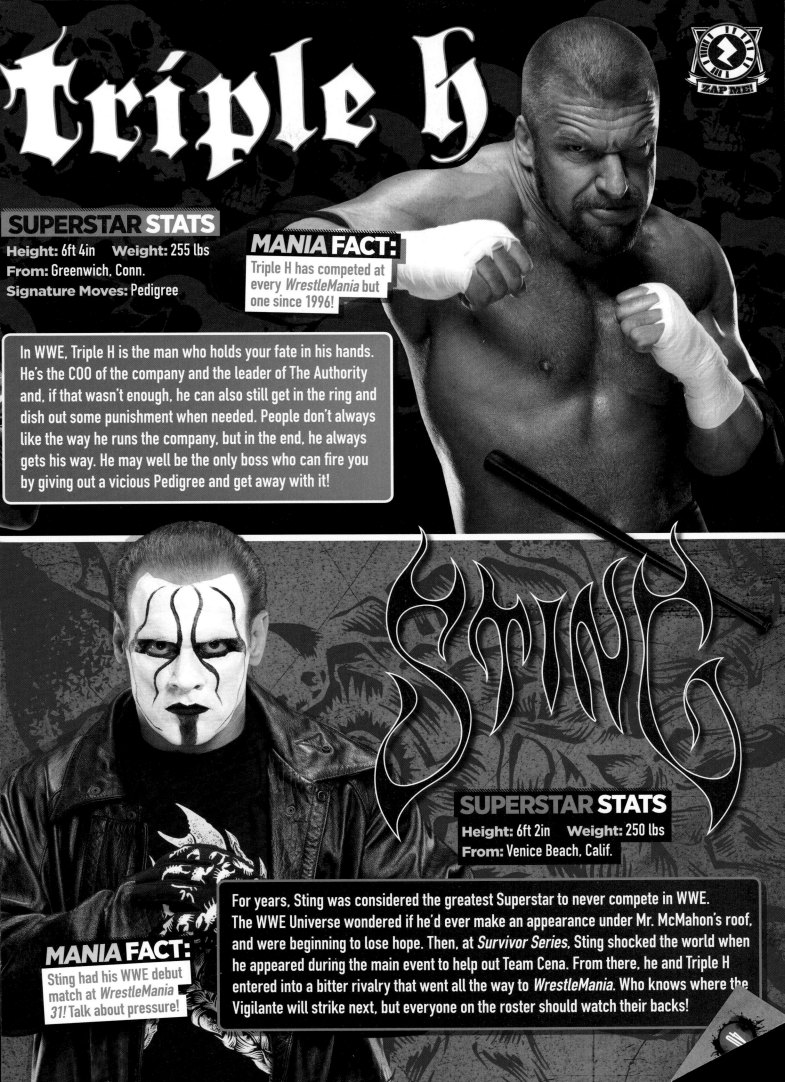

SUPERSTAR STATS

Height: 6ft 4in **Weight:** 255 lbs
From: Greenwich, Conn.
Signature Moves: Pedigree

MANIA FACT:
Triple H has competed at every *WrestleMania* but one since 1996!

In WWE, Triple H is the man who holds your fate in his hands. He's the COO of the company and the leader of The Authority and, if that wasn't enough, he can also still get in the ring and dish out some punishment when needed. People don't always like the way he runs the company, but in the end, he always gets his way. He may well be the only boss who can fire you by giving out a vicious Pedigree and get away with it!

STING

SUPERSTAR STATS

Height: 6ft 2in **Weight:** 250 lbs
From: Venice Beach, Calif.

MANIA FACT:
Sting had his WWE debut match at *WrestleMania 31!* Talk about pressure!

For years, Sting was considered the greatest Superstar to never compete in WWE. The WWE Universe wondered if he'd ever make an appearance under Mr. McMahon's roof, and were beginning to lose hope. Then, at *Survivor Series*, Sting shocked the world when he appeared during the main event to help out Team Cena. From there, he and Triple H entered into a bitter rivalry that went all the way to *WrestleMania*. Who knows where the Vigilante will strike next, but everyone on the roster should watch their backs!

WRESTLEMANIA

TRIPLE H VS STING

For months, the Vigilante had challenged The Game. His run-in at *Survivor Series* spoiled Team Authority's chances at defeating Team Cena. From there, he began playing mind games with the Cerebral Assassin, appearing and then disappearing at random. Finally, the rivalry reached a breaking point when Stephanie slapped Sting live on TV on the *Raw* before *WrestleMania*. When they finally met at the Show of Shows, it had gone from a match to an all-out war!

Sting comes to the ring accompanied by the thundering sounds of Taiko drummers, all wearing Sting's famous facepaint!

Is it Triple H or The Terminator? Either way, Sting is in for a fight! Standing tall alongside T-800 robots and wearing cyborg-style armor, Triple H is ready for battle!

Fans are chanting "You still got it!" at Sting, and it looks like they're right!

Sting has power, but Triple H gets the upper hand! Can he make Sting tap out?

The Scorpion Death Lock is locked in! The Game has nowhere to go! This could be it!

D-Generation X is in the house! They're not going to let their friend Triple H get pushed around!

Sting takes to the air! In one amazing flight from the top rope he takes out all of DX and Triple H too!

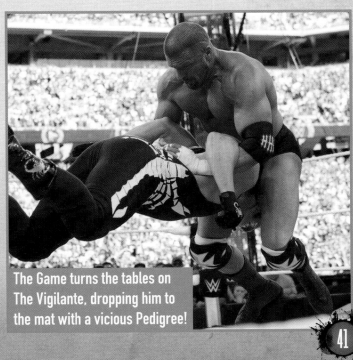

The Game turns the tables on The Vigilante, dropping him to the mat with a vicious Pedigree!

It's hammer time! Unable to pin Sting, Triple H turns to an old friend to get the job done!

First DX...now the nWo are coming out for a piece of the action! This match is an all-new Monday Night War!

The battle outside the ring has given Sting the opening he needs to hit the Scorpion Death Drop! This might be the end for Triple H!

HBK levels the Vigilante with Sweet Chin Music! Sting is outnumbered and outgunned!

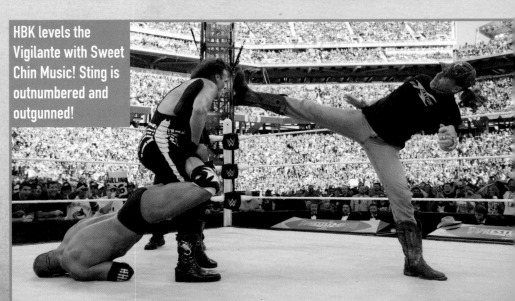

Crack! One swing of Sting's bat and Triple H's hammer is turned into splinters!

Turns out half a hammer is still good enough to take down Sting!

Triple H and his friends celebrate in the ring after an incredible *WrestleMania* victory!

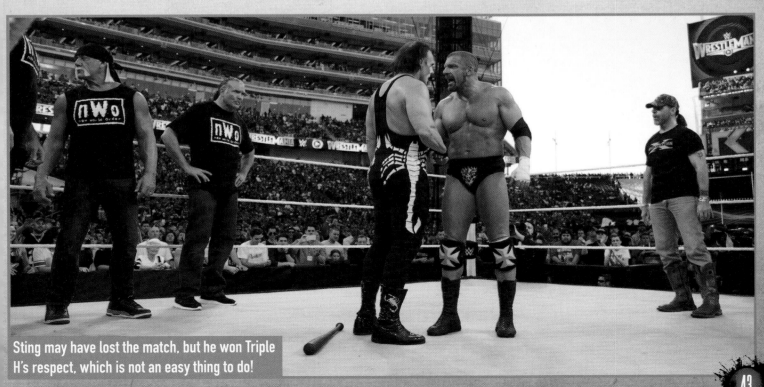

Sting may have lost the match, but he won Triple H's respect, which is not an easy thing to do!

THE BEST OF THE REST!

WrestleMania featured some of the most exciting action and unbelievable surprises ever seen in WWE! Here are just a few of the matches that blew the WWE Universe away!

RANDY ORTON VS SETH ROLLINS

The Viper had been betrayed by Triple H and The Authority, and a Curb Stomp from Seth Rollins put him out of action for months. But at *WrestleMania*, Randy Orton came ready to fight. He battled Seth hard for most of the match, refusing to let the Architect gain the upper hand. The match's most exciting moment came when Rollins attempted to finish Randy with a Curb Stomp, but Orton tossed him into the air and turned the move into a match-ending RKO! Now that's what we call revenge!

ANDRE THE GIANT MEMORIAL BATTLE ROYAL

Big Show wasn't happy about losing to Cesaro in last year's Battle Royal, so at *WrestleMania* this year, he came ready for action! He muscled his way through Superstar after Superstar. After Miz and Damien Mizdow had a major disagreement, the World's Largest Athlete saw his shot. When Damien tossed Miz out, Big Show took advantage and overpowered Mizdow! Andre the Giant was the king of Battle Royals, but there's a new king in town!

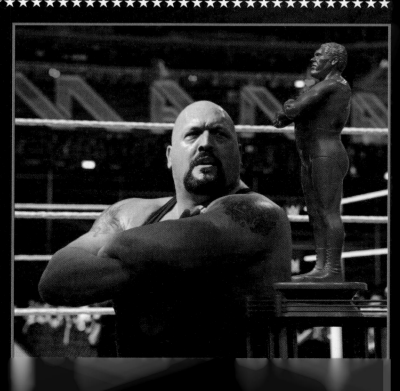

JOHN CENA VS RUSEV

The Super Athlete had spent the last few months running down the United States and telling everyone how superior Russia was to America. And if you know anything about John Cena, you know that nobody trashes the USA when he's around! Cena had had enough of Rusev's trash talking and decided to take the fight right to his front door. It was a brutal battle, with Rusev dishing out as much punishment as he took. But his end came when he accidentally knocked Lana to the floor! Cena used the distraction to nail Rusev with an Attitude Adjustment, scoring a powerful win for the Stars and Stripes!

★★★

LADDER MATCH FOR THE INTERCONTINENTAL CHAMPIONSHIP

WrestleMania was on fire at Levi's Stadium with six Superstars battling it out for Bad News Barrett's Intercontinental Championship! Everyone brought something special to the match. Stardust even brought his own Starbird ladder! In the end, Daniel Bryan and Ziggler traded blows atop the ladder until Bryan knocked Dolph to the mat and unhooked the title for the win! Yes! Yes! Yes!

STENCIL YOURSELF A JOHN CENA T-SHIRT

YOU WILL NEED:
- A THICK PIECE OF CARD
- FABRIC PAINT
- PAINTBRUSH
- PLAIN T-SHIRT
- SCISSORS
- IRON
- MASKING TAPE

1. CUT ALONG THE DOTTED LINE ON THE OPPOSITE PAGE TO REMOVE YOUR CHOSEN DESIGN FROM THE BOOK.

2. STICK THE IMAGE(S) TO A THICK PIECE OF CARD.

3. USING A CRAFT KNIFE OR SCISSORS, CAREFULLY CUT OUT ALL THE BLACK AREAS TO MAKE THE STENCIL HOLES.

4. USING THE MASKING TAPE, STICK YOUR STENCIL TO THE FRONT OF THE T-SHIRT YOU'RE GOING TO CREATE.

5. PAINT THROUGH THE STENCIL ONTO YOUR T-SHIRT, MAKING SURE YOU COVER ALL THE HOLES.

6. SLOWLY AND GENTLY PEEL AWAY THE STENCIL, THEN WAIT FOR THE PAINT TO DRY..

7. IF YOUR PAINT NEEDS TO BE FIXED USING AN IRON, FOLLOW THE INSTRUCTIONS ON THE PACKET. COVER THE PAINT WITH A CLOTH TO STOP IT STICKING TO THE IRON.

WARNING!
KNIVES AND SCISSORS ARE SHARP, AND IRONS ARE HOT! SO ALWAYS ASK AN ADULT FOR HELP!

BE CREATIVE!
ENLARGE YOUR STENCILS ON A PHOTOCOPIER IF YOU WANT TO MAKE THEM BIGGER. YOU CAN ALSO USE MORE THAN ONE STENCIL PER T-SHIRT.

NEVER GIVE UP

NEVER GIVE UP

NOTE: CAREFULLY CUT OUT THE 'C' FROM THIS STENCIL AND HOLD IT IN PLACE ON THE T-SHIRT AS YOU PAINT AROUND IT.

THAT'S A SUPERSTAR FACT!

Think you've got all the facts on your favourite WWE Superstars? We've got some tidbits that will surprise and amaze you and your friends! Your challenge is to match up the Superstar with their fact.

FACT 1
When I'm not competing in WWE, I am the lead singer in my own rock band!

WHO?

FACT 2
I'm not only an expert in the ring, I'm also an expert on SpongeBob SquarePants trivia!

WHO?

FACT 3
Before I was in WWE, my face was all over MTV! I was a star on the shows *The Real World* and *Road Rules* before I stepped between the ropes!

WHO?

FACT 4
Before I was a WWE Superstar, in college, I was a superstar basketball player!

WHO?

FACT 5
I can insult you in five different languages. I'm fluent in English, German, Italian, French and Romanish!!

WHO?

BAD NEWS BARRETT   **JOHN CENA**   **ROMAN REIGNS**   **SETH ROLLINS**   **THE ROCK**   **DOLPH ZIGGLER**

FACT 6

When I'm not out ruining Superstars' days or competing for the Intercontinental Championship, I'm a die-hard supporter of Preston North End!

WHO?

FACT 7

On top of being a Money in the Bank winner, I also own my own wrestling school!

WHO?

FACT 8

I ruled the ring in my day, but I could have ruled rock and roll just as easily! I'm a skilled bass player who once auditioned for the Rolling Stones!

WHO?

FACT 9

I might not show any fear in the ring or on the screen, but I am scared of spiders!

WHO?

FACT 10

On top of my collection of WWE titles, I also have an extensive collection of lunch boxes!

WHO?

FACT 11

It's no wonder I'm a two-time Divas Champion. Both of my parents were wrestlers and I made my in-ring debut when I was 13!

WHO?

FACT 12

I may be the face of WWE today, but before I rose to greatness, I was known as The Prototype!

WHO?

FACT 13

Before coming to WWE, I had a brief run in the NFL, playing for the Minnesota Vikings and the Jacksonville Jaguars!

WHO?

So you think you did well? Is that a fact? Check your answers on page 60 to see if you really are a Superstar know it all!

BATISTA //// CESARO //// THE MIZ //// PAIGE //// BIG SHOW //// CHRIS JERICHO //// HULK HOGAN

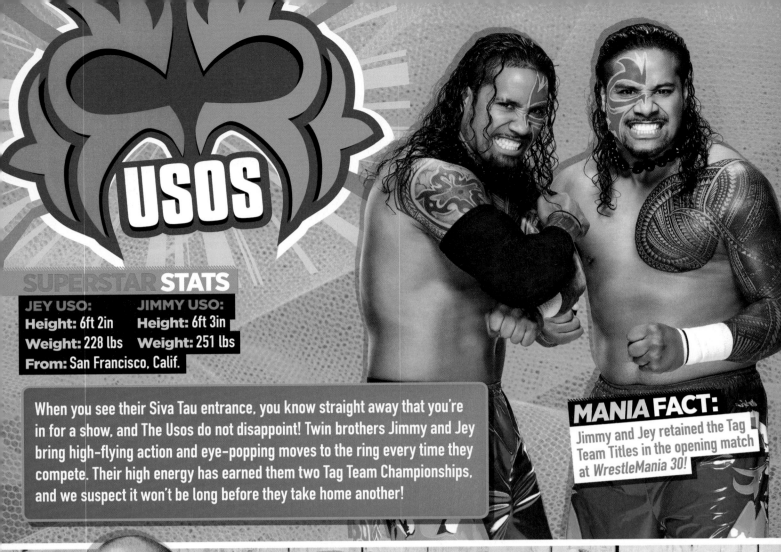

USOS

SUPERSTAR STATS

JEY USO:
Height: 6ft 2in
Weight: 228 lbs
From: San Francisco, Calif.

JIMMY USO:
Height: 6ft 3in
Weight: 251 lbs

When you see their Siva Tau entrance, you know straight away that you're in for a show, and The Usos do not disappoint! Twin brothers Jimmy and Jey bring high-flying action and eye-popping moves to the ring every time they compete. Their high energy has earned them two Tag Team Championships, and we suspect it won't be long before they take home another!

MANIA FACT:
Jimmy and Jey retained the Tag Team Titles in the opening match at *WrestleMania 30!*

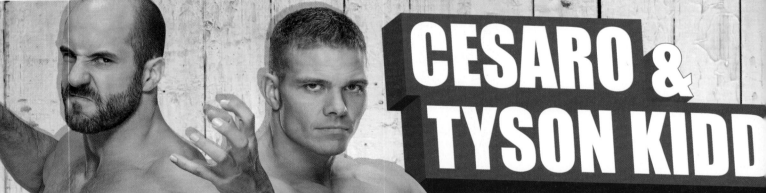

CESARO & TYSON KIDD

MANIA FACT:
Cesaro made waves at *WrestleMania 30* by tossing out Big Show to win the first-ever Andre the Giant Memorial Battle Royal! A year later, he and Kidd retained their Tag Team Titles during the *WrestleMania* pre-show.

SUPERSTAR STATS

CESARO:
Height: 6ft 5in
Weight: 232 lbs
From: Lucerne, Switzerland

TYSON KIDD:
Height: 5ft 10in
Weight: 195 lbs
From: Calgary, Alberta, Canada

When you see Cesaro and Tyson Kidd in action, you wonder why they didn't get together sooner! Tyson was trained in Stu Hart's legendary Dungeon wrestling school, while Cesaro brings his top-notch athleticism to every match. Tyson's Sharpshooter combined with Cesaro's swing is as lethal a finishing combo as anyone could ask for! Separately these two were tough competitors. Together, they are double the trouble!

THE ASCENSION

SUPERSTAR STATS

KONNOR:
Height: 6ft 4in
Weight: 265 lbs
From: Grand Rapids, Mich.
Signature Move: Fall of Man

VIKTOR:
Height: 6ft 2in
Weight: 219 lbs
From: Calgary, Alberta, Canada.

The Ascension feed on destruction, and they are always hungry! After making their debut on *Raw* by laying waste to The Miz and Damien Mizdow, Konnor and Viktor promised to pave a path of destruction through WWE, and that's just what they've been doing. It remains to be seen if there's anyone out there who has what it takes to take out these powerhouses for good!

MANIA FACT:

Konnor and Viktor made their *WrestleMania* debuts by competing in the Andre the Giant Battle Royal. Unfortunately, they lost to Big Show.

NEW DAY

KOFI KINGSTON:
Height: 6ft 0in
Weight: 212 lbs
From: Ghana, West Africa
Signature move: Trouble in Paradise Africa

BIG E:
Height: 5ft 11in
Weight: 290 lbs
From: Tampa, Fla.
Signature move: The Big Ending

XAVIER WOODS:
Height: 5ft 11in
Weight: 205 lbs
From: Atlanta
Signature moves: Honor Roll; Lost in the Woods

MANIA FACT:

The New Day kicked off *WrestleMania 31* in a Fatal Four Way tag match, but failed to win the titles. They took home the gold a month later, defeating Tyson Kidd and Cesaro at Extreme Rules.

As Kofi Kingston, Xavier Woods and Big E, they were not making much of an impact, but as The New Day, they are already making waves. They made a strong showing right out of the gate, defeating Goldust and Stardust in the kick-off match at TLC 2014. From there they went on a winning streak that eventually came to an end at the *Royal Rumble*. The New Day are all about power and respect. With the way they've been handling themselves in the ring, they've got plenty of both!

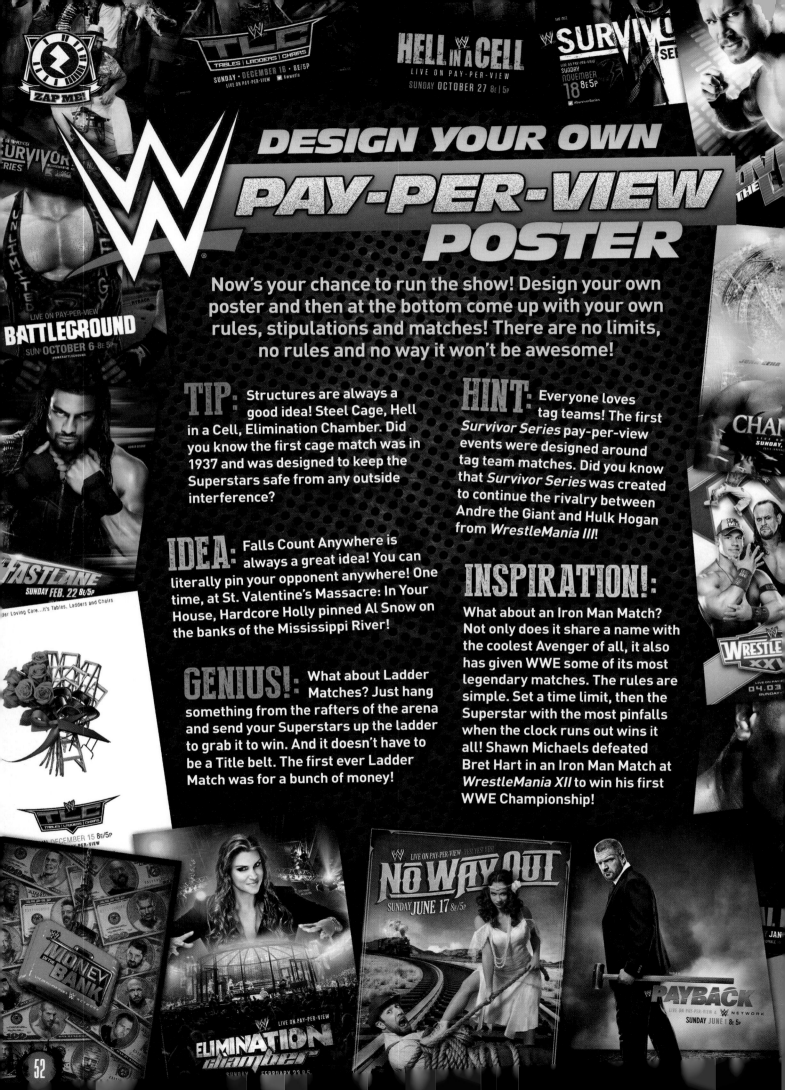

DESIGN YOUR OWN PAY-PER-VIEW POSTER

Now's your chance to run the show! Design your own poster and then at the bottom come up with your own rules, stipulations and matches! There are no limits, no rules and no way it won't be awesome!

TIP: Structures are always a good idea! Steel Cage, Hell in a Cell, Elimination Chamber. Did you know the first cage match was in 1937 and was designed to keep the Superstars safe from any outside interference?

HINT: Everyone loves tag teams! The first *Survivor Series* pay-per-view events were designed around tag team matches. Did you know that *Survivor Series* was created to continue the rivalry between Andre the Giant and Hulk Hogan from *WrestleMania III*!

IDEA: Falls Count Anywhere is always a great idea! You can literally pin your opponent anywhere! One time, at St. Valentine's Massacre: In Your House, Hardcore Holly pinned Al Snow on the banks of the Mississippi River!

INSPIRATION!: What about an Iron Man Match? Not only does it share a name with the coolest Avenger of all, it also has given WWE some of its most legendary matches. The rules are simple. Set a time limit, then the Superstar with the most pinfalls when the clock runs out wins it all! Shawn Michaels defeated Bret Hart in an Iron Man Match at *WrestleMania XII* to win his first WWE Championship!

GENIUS!: What about Ladder Matches? Just hang something from the rafters of the arena and send your Superstars up the ladder to grab it to win. And it doesn't have to be a Title belt. The first ever Ladder Match was for a bunch of money!

WWE BIG QUIZ

PART THREE

Can you identify what's happening in these extreme close ups? We've given you some hints to help you out!

Q1: WE LOVE TO MAKE AN ENTRANCE, AND WE ESPECIALLY LOVE IT WHEN YOU JOIN IN! CAN YOU GUESS WHO WE ARE?

Q2: I MAY BE A NEWCOMER HERE IN WWE, BUT I'M STILL A LEGEND!

Q3: I LIKE TO FIGHT BECAUSE I'M A WARRIOR! KNOW WHO I AM?

Q4: YOU HAVE TO FIGHT REAL HARD TO GET ME. AND YOU'LL HAVE TO GUESS REAL HARD TO FIGURE OUT WHAT I AM!

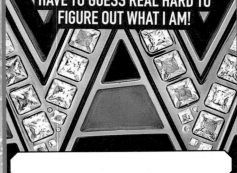

Q5: I WAITED FOR MY MOMENT TO WIN BIG AT *WRESTLEMANIA*. BUT I WOULDN'T WAIT TO FIGURE THIS OUT IF I WERE YOU!

Q6: THINK YOU CAN SEE ME? GIVE IT YOUR BEST SHOT!

Q7: YOU'LL HAVE TO LOOK CLOSE TO FIND OUT WHO I AM, AND YOU MAY NOT LIKE WHAT YOU FIND!

Q8: THIS WAS ONE EPIC *WRESTLEMANIA* BATTLE, AND IT'LL BE PRETTY EPIC FOR YOU IF YOU CAN FIGURE IT OUT!

Q9: YOU'LL BE PUMPING YOUR FISTS LIKE US IF YOU CAN FIGURE OUT WHO WE ARE!

Q10: THIS MATCH WAS ONE OF THE WILDEST EVER SEEN AT *WRESTLEMANIA*! ARE YOU WILD ENOUGH TO GUESS WHICH ONE IT IS?

Q11: SEE IF YOU CAN GRAB THIS CHALLENGE BY THE HORNS AND GUESS WHO I AM!

Q12: WHAT WILL YOU FOLLOW TO FIND OUT WHO I AM?

Q13: LOOK TO THE STARS! THE ANSWER IS THERE!

Q14: THIS IS THE BIGGEST DAY OF THE YEAR, AT LEAST, UNTIL THE DAY YOU FIGURE OUT THIS CLUE!

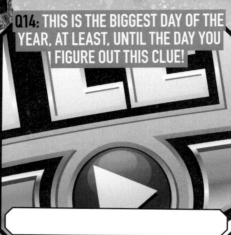

Q15: TAKE A GOOD LOOK AND SEE IF YOU CAN GUESS WHO I AM. BUT NOT TOO CLOSE OR YOU MIGHT GET A SNAKE BITE!

Q16: YOU DON'T HAVE TO BE SUPER OR AN ATHLETE TO GUESS THIS ONE. BUT IT MIGHT HELP!

Q17: YOU WANT ME TO FEED YOU THE ANSWER? NO WAY!

Q18: YOU'RE ON A WINNING STREAK! CAN YOU KEEP IT GOING?

Q19: THINK YOU KNOW WHO I AM? YOU'LL HAVE TO DOUBLE YOUR SMARTS!

Q20: IF YOU GUESS THIS ONE, YOU'LL BE SAYING 'YES!' FOR DAYS!

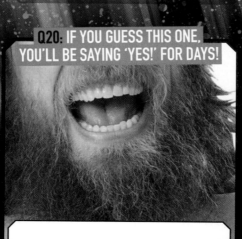

Are you Superstar material? Tally up all your answers from part 1, 2 and 3 on **page 60** to see which WWE personality you line up with!

RANDY ORTON

SUPERSTAR STATS

Height: 6ft 5in   Weight: 235 lbs
From: St. Louis, Mo.   Signature Move: RKO

Randy Orton is the Viper, but that doesn't necessarily mean he's all bad. It just means that, if you mess with him, you might get bitten! Making a surprise return at *Fastlane* to deal out RKOs to Kane and J&J Security, Orton turned against The Authority and went out on his own. Now there's a snake on the loose in the WWE locker room and everyone had better watch out!

MANIA FACT:
Randy Orton became Undertaker's 13th victim at the Show of Shows, falling to the Deadman at *WrestleMania 21* in 2005!

SUPERSTAR STATS

Height: 6ft 1in   Weight: 217 lbs
From: Davenport, Iowa.   Signature Move: Curb Stomp

MANIA FACT:
Seth Rollins is the first Superstar to ever cash in the Money in the Bank briefcase at *WrestleMania*. The Architect shocked the WWE Universe by pinning Roman Reigns to conclude *WrestleMania 31* at Levi's Stadium!

They call Seth Rollins The Architect, and it's a fitting name, because he always has a plan. When he betrayed his former friend Roman Reigns and Dean Ambrose, breaking up The Shield, Seth revealed that he had been plotting to do it from the beginning. Since splitting from The Shield, Seth has blazed a new path, winning the Money in the Bank briefcase, becoming one of The Authority's most trusted members and stealing the WWE World Heavyweight Championship on the Grandest Stage. The Architect, it seems, is building a legendary career.

SUPERSTAR STATS

Height: 7ft 0in **Weight:** 425 lbs
From: Tampa, Fla.
Signature Moves: Chokeslam; KO Punch; Colossal Clutch

Big Show has been an active Superstar for 20 years, and he's still going stronger than ever. With his devastating KO punch, it is no surprise that The Authority recruited him to do their bidding. For several months, he pounded his way through anyone who dared challenge Triple H and Stephanie McMahon like a one-man wrecking crew. At the rate he's going, he could have another 20 years of destruction left in him!

MANIA FACT:
Big Show competed in WWE's only Sumo Match, facing Akebono in a losing effort at *WrestleMania 21!*

DEAN AMBROSE

SUPERSTAR STATS

Height: 6ft 4in **Weight:** 225 lbs
From: Cincinnati, Ohio.
Signature Move: Dirty Deeds

The best thing about Dean Ambrose is you never know what he's going to do next! Of course, for Superstars going against him, that's probably the worst thing. Just ask Seth Rollins, who was so fed up with Dean's random attacks, he started having him banned from arenas! More recently, he made life difficult for Bad News Barrett, by stealing the Intercontinental Title from him and claiming it for himself. Dean is totally unpredictable. The only thing you can expect from him is the unexpected!

MANIA FACT:
It was Dean Ambrose's stealing of Bad News Barrett's Intercontinental Title that led to the announcement of a Ladder Match at *WrestleMania 31!*

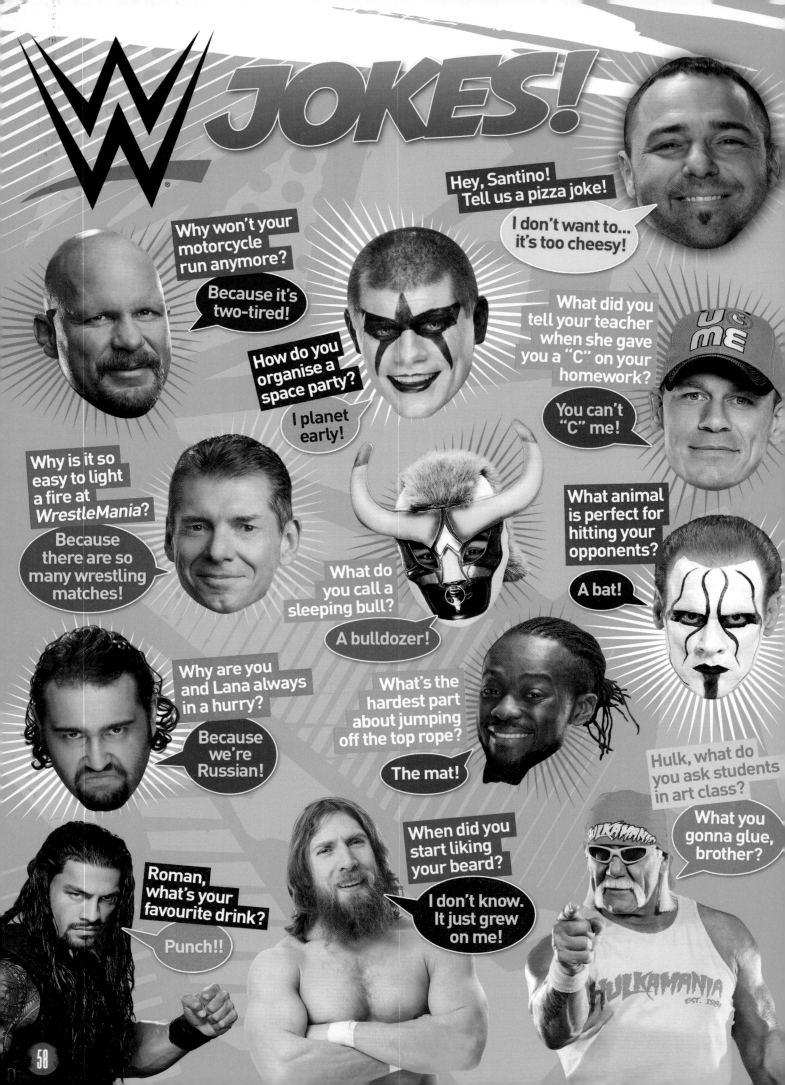

FINAL CHALLENGE!

Hold on a second, Hulkamaniacs! You've done a great job, but there's one last riddle to solve! Someone has secretly hidden these 15 objects around the book! Go back through and see how many you can find. Then come back here and solve the riddle to uncover the identity of the sneaky Superstar who hid the objects!

ERIC ROWAN'S SHEEP MASK

BUNNY

JBL'S COWBOY HAT

TAG TEAM TITLE

JOHN CENA'S HAT

THE MIZ'S SUNGLASSES

SIN CARA'S MAKS

SHEAMUS'S CELTIC CROSS

STING'S BASEBALL BAT

BRAY WYATT'S ROCKING CHAIR

DIVA TITLE

TRIPLE H'S SLEDGEHAMMER

TRIPLE H'S WRESTLEMANIA MASK

MONEY IN THE BANK BRIEFCASE

KANE'S MASK

Here's a hint, brother! To solve this clue, letters equal numbers! So, "A" equals "1," "B" equals "2," and so on!

RIDDLE 19, 5, 20, 8, 18, 15, 12, 12, 9, 14, 19

ANSWER ....

Turn the page to reveal the answer.

ANSWERS

PAGES 18-19: BIG QUIZ PART 1

01 San Diego
02 Mr. McMahon
03 WrestleMania IX against Giant Gonzalez
04 The Nexus
05 Shawn Michaels
06 COO
07 Hands Off the Top Rope Match
08 Honky Tonk Man
09 Buzzards
10 Seth Rollins
11 Stunt Double
12 15 times
13 Pinfall or submission
14 Andre the Giant
15 Anoa'i
16 Yokozuna
17 Shawn Michaels
18 Triple H
19 Randy Savage
20 Alberto Del Rio

PAGE 23: FROM THE OFFICE OF THE AUTHORITY

01 Seth Rollins
02 Daniel Bryan
03 Bad News Barrett
04 Bray Wyatt
05 Dean Ambrose
06 The Rock
07 Randy Orton
08 Sheamus

PAGES 24-25: SUPERSTAR SWAP

JOHN CENA
Shirt: Bray Wyatt
Trunks: Ryback
Boots: Sheamus

ROMAN REIGNS
Shirt: Ryback
Trunks: Sheamus
Boots: Seth Rollins

BRAY WYATT
Shirt: Sheamus
Trunks: John Cena
Boots: Stardust

STARDUST
Shirt: John Cena
Trunks: Seth Rollins
Boots: Adam Rose

SETH ROLLINS
Shirt: Adam Rose
Trunks: Stardust
Boots: Roman Reigns

RYBACK
Shirt: Stardust
Trunks: Adam Rose
Boots: Bray Wyatt

SHEAMUS
Shirt: Seth Rollins
Trunks: Roman Reigns
Boots: John Cena

ADAM ROSE
Shirt: Roman Reigns
Trunks: Bray Wyatt
Boots: Ryback

PAGES 32-33: FACES OF THE UNDERTAKER

1990 Mortician
1994 Original Deadman
1995 The Phantom
1996 Lord of Darkness
1998 WrestleMania XIV
1999 Minister of Evil
2001 American Badass
2003 Big Evil
2004 Return of the Deadman
2013 The Last Outlaw

PAGES 34-35: BIG QUIZ PART 2

01 FALSE. *He has never won the Intercontinental Title*
02 TRUE
03 FALSE. *WrestleMania VI and WrestleMania X8 were held in Canada.*
04 FALSE. *He first won the WWE Championship in 2002.*
05 TRUE.
06 TRUE. *He pinned Bobby Lashley at Backlash 2007.*
07 FALSE. *Sting has yet to win any Title in WWE.*
08 TRUE.
09 TRUE.
10 FALSE. *Linda McMahon never held a Title.*
11 TRUE

PAGES 34-35: BIG QUIZ PART 2 CONT...

12 FALSE. *Several Superstars have wrestled multiple matches at the same 'Mania, including Randy Savage, Bret Hart and Ted DiBiase.*
13 FALSE. *He only held the title nine times in his career.*
14 TRUE
15 TRUE. *Bo was born in 1990, Paige in 1992.*
16 TRUE. *The 1992 Rumble was the only event in which the winner of the Royal Rumble also walked away with the title.*
17 TRUE. *The promoter set up chicken wire around the ring to keep the wrestlers in and the fans out!*
18 FALSE. *While mostly a vegetarian, Daniel does eat some meat in order to keep up with the physically demanding life of a WWE Superstar.*
19 TRUE
20 TRUE. *He portrayed his legendary dad on an episode of That 70's Show.*

PAGES 36-37: SUPERSTAR WORDSEARCH

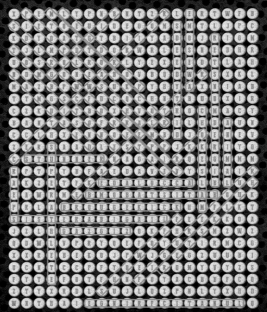

EXTRA CHALLENGE

Rattlesnake **Stunner**
People's Champ **Rock Bottom**
Lunatic Fringe **Dirty Deeds**
Deadman **Tombstone**
Eater of Worlds **Sister Abigail**
Hulkster **Leg Drop**
Animal **Batista Bomb**
Super Athlete **Accolade**
Awesome **Figure Four**
Big Dog **Spear**
Showoff **Zig Zag**
Viper **RKO**
Big Red Monster **Chokeslam**
Celtic Warrior **Brogue Kick**

PAGES 48-49: THAT'S A SUPERSTAR FACT

FACT 1 Chris Jericho
FACT 2 Dolph Ziggler
FACT 3 The Miz
FACT 4 Big Show
FACT 5 Cesaro
FACT 6 Bad News Barrett
FACT 7 Seth Rollins
FACT 8 Hulk Hogan
FACT 9 The Rock
FACT 10 Batista
FACT 11 Paige
FACT 12 John Cena
FACT 13 Roman Reigns

PAGES 54-55: BIG QUIZ PART 3

01 The Usos
02 Sting
03 Sheamus
04 WWE World Heavyweight Championsip
05 Seth Rollins
06 John Cena
07 Bray Wyatt
08 Roman Reigns vs Brock Lesnar
09 Lucha Dragons
10 Intercontinental Title Ladder Match
11 El Torito
12 Erick Rowan
13 Stardust
14 *WrestleMaina 31*
15 Randy Orton
16 Rusev
17 Ryback
18 Undertaker
19 Nikki Bella
20 Daniel Bryan

HOW DID YOU DO ON THE BIG QUIZ?

0-10: DOINK THE CLOWN
Whoops! Looks like you've been too busy clowning about when you should have been brushing up on your WWE knowledge!

11-20: SANTINO MARELLA
Not bad. You're kind of a goofball, but you've still been paying attention from time to time!

21-30: MANKIND
Pretty good! You may have fallen through a table or two, but you still managed to put up a decent showing!

31-40: RANDY ORTON
Nice work! You may have taken some beatings here and there, but you're too smart to stay down for long. Your wits always see you through!

41-50: ROMAN REIGNS
Alright! You're tough as nails, and you don't know the meaning of the word quit!

51-60: JOHN CENA
Fantastic! You're the champ, the tops, the true king of the ring!

PAGES 59: FINAL CHALLENGE

SETH ROLLINS

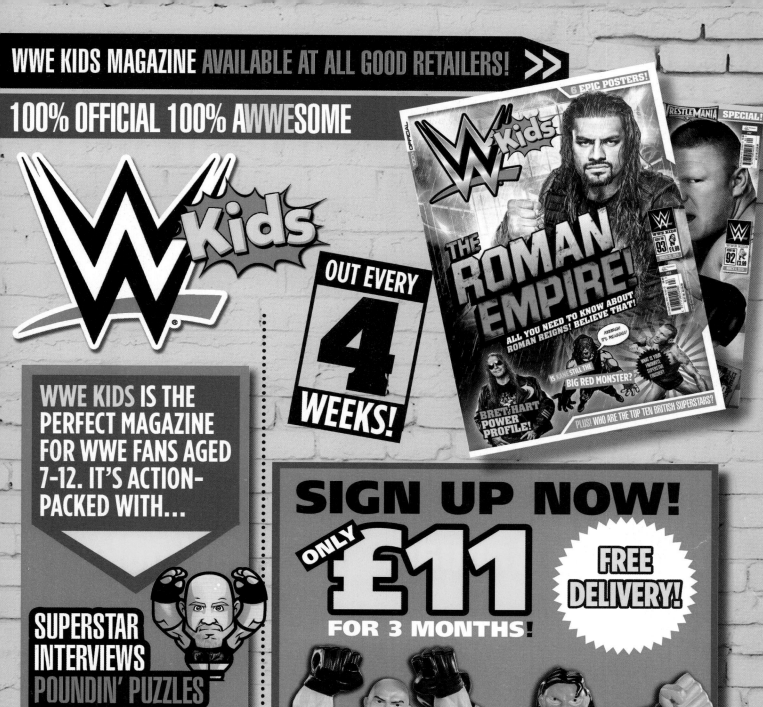

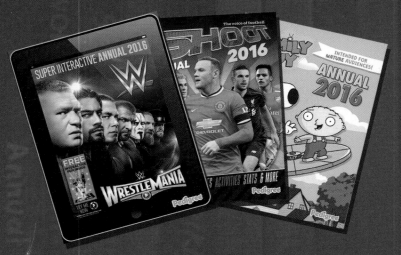

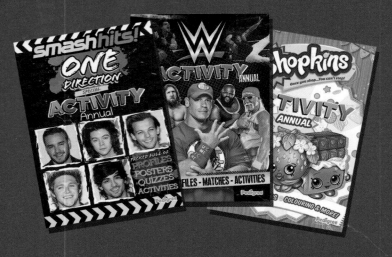
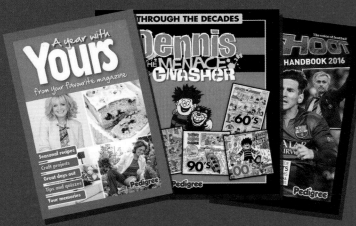